THINKING
ABOUT HINDUISM

World Religions General Editor: Raymond F. Trudgian
International Secretary Christian Education Movement

THINKING ABOUT HINDUISM

ERIC J. SHARPE

*Senior Lecturer in Religious Studies,
University of Lancaster*

LUTTERWORTH EDUCATIONAL

First published 1971

Lutterworth Educational

The quotations from the Bhagavad Gita are reproduced with the permission of J. M. Dent and Sons from *Hindu Scriptures* (Everyman's Library): Text translated by R. C. Zaehner.

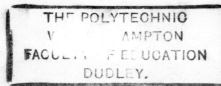
ISBN 0 7188 1822 9

Copyright © 1971 Eric J. Sharpe

Printed in Great Britain by
Cox & Wyman Ltd., London, Fakenham and Reading

CONTENTS

List of Illustrations		7
Editor's Introduction		9
1. INDIA AND THE BEGINNINGS OF HINDUISM		11
Size and Population		11
What Does the Word 'Hinduism' Mean?		13
How did Hinduism Start?		14
The Indus Culture		16
2. SCRIPTURES AND GODS		19
Revealed Scripture		19
Traditional Scripture		21
The Great Gods		25
3. THE SEARCH FOR KNOWLEDGE		28
The Belief in Transmigration		29
The Belief in Karma		29
The Belief in Maya		30
The Practice of Yoga		31
4. STORIES OF GODS AND MEN		33
The Role of the Pandit		34
The Bhagavad Gita		34
5. WORSHIP IN HOME AND TEMPLE		38
The Temple Priest		38
The Household Priest		41
The Guru		41
The Pandit		41
The Swami		41
Worship in the Home		41
Worship in the Temple		44
Pilgrimages		46

6. WHAT IS A HINDU?   47
   Class and Caste   47
   Rebirth   49
   The Cow   50
   Vegetarianism   51
   Religious Equality   51

7. HINDUISM IN THE MODERN WORLD   53
   The Brahma Samaj   54
   The Arya Samaj   55
   The Theosophical Society   55
   Shri Ramakrishna   55
   Swami Vivekananda   56
   Other Leaders   56
   Mohandas Karamchand Gandhi   58
   Postscript   60

LIST OF ILLUSTRATIONS

1. Hindu Temple, Delhi
2. Indus Civilization Sites
3. Shiva Nataraja, Lord of the Dance
4. Hindu Temple in Madras showing intricate carvings
5. A worshipper of Vishnu, wearing the mark of the Shri-Vaishnava Sect on his forehead
6. Nandi, the White Bull on which the God Shiva is believed to ride
7. A Sannyasin (holy man) practising Yoga
8. Image of Shri Ramakrishna in the meditation hall of Ramakrishna Mission, Bombay
9. Bathing Ghats on the River Ganges at Hardwar
10. Funeral pyre on the river bank
11. On a pilgrimage
12. Cows in a street in Madras
13. Gandhi at a reception given by Rabindranath Tagore
14. 'Mahatma' Gandhi

For permission to reproduce the above photographs the author and publishers are indebted to the Keystone Press Agency (for numbers 4, 10, 12, 14), to the Camera Press Agency (for numbers 1, 9, 11, 13) to Thames and Hudson (number 2 from Sir Mortimer Wheeler's *Civilizations of the Indus Valley and Beyond*) to Atlantis Verlag, Switzerland (for numbers 5 and 7 from Martin Hurlimann's *India*) to Paul Hamlyn (for numbers 3 and 6 from V. Ions' *Indian Mythology*). Number 8 is by the author.

EDITOR'S INTRODUCTION

The teaching of World Religions has taken a place in religious education in this country for some time. Often however, it was left until the sixth form when a rapid survey of at least two or three religions per term was made. At the end pupils were expected to 'compare' these with Christianity. The most that could be hoped for in such a situation was an acquaintance with the historical founder of a particular faith and knowledge of the more unusual customs and traditions associated with their followers who were thought of as living in some other part of the world.

In recent years the situation has changed so dramatically that a new approach is called for. Not only are many of those faiths now represented in our schools, but mosques and temples form a communal focal point for new immigrants as the synagogues have done for immigrants of another era. Even in areas where the other faiths are not represented the situation presents searching questions through newspaper items and television documentaries.

Long before the sixth form therefore a majority of children will have some knowledge of other religions through their own community or the mass media. For an increasing number this knowledge begins in the primary school.

It follows that the school leaver and certainly the student teacher in a college of education will want to look more deeply at a religion other than their own. Ideally at this stage time should be given to one faith only or students could follow a thematic study through the beliefs of the main world religions. Themes such as the Nature of God, the meaning of worship, the problem of evil and suffering, war and peace are but a few of the rewarding studies which could be carried out. In this way some approach can be made to another culture, another faith which will provide both understanding and enrichment in preparation for living in the plural society.

This series of 'Thinking about' books is presented with this need in mind. Each booklet deals with one faith only and the text has been prepared by a member of that faith or by Christians of deep sensitivity who have brought their awareness of the religious dimension and their academic training to a presentation of a sympathetic portrayal of another faith.

Not only do these books deal with matters of theology and practice but also the social and political implications of each living faith are drawn out for the reader. It is true that we can never begin fully to understand another faith until we have lived for some time in the country where that faith is practised by the majority of people. It is hoped that these books will begin the quest and be related to the search for truth in such disciplines as geography, as we try to understand why particular countries have adopted a certain faith; in history, as we see man searching for an identity often motivated by religion, and in social studies as we see how mankind has sought to live in meaningful communities.

Apart from their educational value this series is presented in the hope that it will play its part in enhancing community relations in this country. It is some time now since the Rt. Hon. Roy Jenkins when he was Home Secretary defined integration as 'not a flattening process to produce "carbon copies" of Englishmen, but equal opportunity accompanied by cultural diversity in an atmosphere of mutual tolerance.'

This book seeks to bring that tolerance to the cultural and religious diversity in our society in the hope that whatever the faith of the readers they will understand their own faith at a deeper level as through this book they come into contact with another world faith, and that through their study they will develop a deeper and wider conception of religion.

As a member of the Advisory team of the Christian Education Movement with special responsibility for advising teachers and pupils on the study of World Religions I trust that this series will go some way to help the need which is daily expressed in our mail by teachers, student teachers and pupils alike.

Annandale, 1971

1

INDIA AND THE BEGINNINGS OF HINDUISM

The first and most important thing to be said about Hinduism is that it is connected very closely with India and with the Indian way of life. Hinduism can of course be called a religion, in that Hindus believe certain things. We might also say that Hinduism includes many religions, since Hindus do not all believe exactly the same things. What we shall try to do is to ask what Hindus actually believe, and to show how their beliefs affect some of the things they do.

All Indians are not Hindus and not all Hindus are to be found in India. Yet the story of Hinduism is so closely bound up with the land and life of India that it is scarcely possible to understand the one without understanding the other.

Size and Population

The **area** of India is about one and a quarter million square miles, or about twelve times the size of Great Britain. The area of the United States of America is more than twice that of India.

The **population** of India in 1961 was approximately 442 millions, and since then it has grown to well over 500 millions. The problem of poverty, and the difficulty of feeding such a large population, are well known. Many parts of India are almost waterless for months on end, and the failure of the monsoon rains often means famine. At the present time there are almost ten times as many people in India as there are in Great Britain, and two and a half times as many as there are in the United States. In terms of population, there is only one larger country in the world and that is China.

In spite of this enormous population, there are only seven cities in India

1. Hindu Temple, Delhi

with more than a million inhabitants. These (in alphabetical order) are Ahmedabad, Bangalore, Bombay, Calcutta, Delhi, Hyderabad and Madras. In 1961, 82 per cent of the people were listed as 'rural', i.e., living in villages and small towns and making their living mainly from agriculture.

At the last census, 85 per cent of the people (or more than 375 millions) were shown to be Hindus. This means that if we count only the Hindus in India, there are over seven times as many Hindus as there are people in Great Britain. Other important religious groups in India include Muslims (10%), Christians (2·3%) and Sikhs (1·7%).

India is a country of many languages. There are fourteen main ones and literally hundreds of smaller ones (spoken by smaller numbers of people). One of India's major problems is that people living in the north who speak languages like Hindi and Bengali are unable to communicate with Indians from the south whose language is Tamil or Telegu. English is still widely spoken, however.

India was part of the British Empire from 1858 until 1947. When independence came, Muslims in the north of India were able to form their own state, Pakistan, the religion of which was to be the rigidly exclusive Islam. The new state of India became officially secular, acknowledging the equality of all religions. This decision was perhaps the only way of putting an end to the bitter religious conflict between Hindus and Muslims in the north, but it divided India, and has often been criticized by Hindus who feel that their sacred motherland was torn apart by this decision.

These are just a few of the facts which we should remember when talking about the religions of India, and about Hinduism.

What Does the Word 'Hinduism' Mean?

Some religions have names that refer back to their founders. Christianity, for instance, refers back to Jesus Christ and Buddhism to Gautama Buddha. It is therefore possible to talk about these religions in terms of what their founders taught. Islam (which really means 'obedience') has sometimes been called Muhammadanism for the same reason, after its founder Muhammad.

The words 'Hindu' and 'Hinduism' do not, however, refer to a teacher. They referred originally to a place on the map, the land around the River Indus (see map). In the Middle Ages, when Muslim invaders began to penetrate into the north-west of India, they called those people who were not converted to Islam 'Hindus'. It was only gradually that the people of India themselves began to use the word to describe their own religion, following the example of Europeans, who took over the word from the

Persian language. Even today many Hindus have probably never heard the word 'Hindu' and have no name for their own religion.

So Hinduism really means nothing less than the traditional religion of India in one form or another. It does not describe one single group of beliefs and practices, but many such groups. We shall see that the beliefs of Hindus, although they have some things in common, vary greatly. A Hindu may believe in one God or many gods; his faith may be very simple or very complicated. There are Hindus who observe many of the ancient traditions, and others who do not – 'conservative' or 'orthodox' Hindus and 'liberal' or 'modern' Hindus as we might call them. We shall try to see what are the differences between them as we go on. For the present we can say that a Hindu is someone who is *born into* the traditional Indian pattern of society, with all its beliefs and practices, and who has done nothing to step outside that pattern, for instance, by being converted to Islam or Christianity. 'Hinduism' is the word we use to describe both the traditional religion and the traditional social structure of India. (On the caste system, see p. 47.)

How did Hinduism Start?

Hinduism did not start with the teachings of a prophet or holy man. Unlike the other great religions of the world, such as Christianity, Buddhism and Islam, the beliefs and practices of Hinduism do not go back to the teachings of a single founder. This is not to say that Hinduism has no saints or holy men. On the contrary, it has many, and their teachings are followed with great care and reverence, but none of these can be called a founder.

Hinduism (although we must remember that it has not always been called by that name) is as old as Indian civilization, and there is an unbroken line of tradition reaching back almost five thousand years in time, to about 3000 B.C. We cannot see Hinduism starting at that time; in fact we cannot see Hinduism 'starting' at all. But however far back we look into the history of India we can see men and women worshipping gods and goddesses, and behaving in ways we can recognize as 'Hindu'.

We may say, then, that Hinduism began (as all religion began) with a sense of dependence upon unseen powers. These were thought to control birth, life and death, the fertility of man, beast and field. As times change, the sense of dependence changes. In the modern world, people feel more dependent on money and machines and politicians than upon the forces of nature. But in the India of five thousand years ago, when people relied entirely on agriculture for their needs, when the expectation of life was

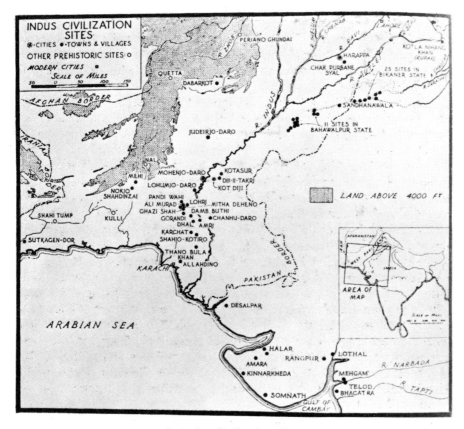

The map contains the following labels:

INDUS CIVILIZATION SITES
⊛·CITIES ●·TOWNS & VILLAGES
OTHER PREHISTORIC SITES: ○
MODERN CITIES ■
SCALE OF MILES
50 0 50 100 150

AFGHAN BORDER

PERIANO GHUNDAI

QUETTA
DABARKOT

HARAPPA
KOTLA NIHANG KHAN (RUPAR)
CHAK PURBANE SYAL
25 SITES IN BIKANER STATE
SANDHANAWALA

JUDEIRJO-DARO
11 SITES IN BAHAWALPUR STATE

NAL
MEHI
MOHENJO-DARO
KOTASUR
DIJI-II-TAKRI
NOKJO SHAHDINZAI
LOHUMJO-DARO
KOT DIJI
PANDI WAHI
ALI MURAD
LOHRI
MITHA DEHENO
GHAZI SHAH
DAMB BUTHI
SHAHI TUMP
KULLI
GORANDI
CHANHU-DARO
DHAL
AMRI
KARCHAT
SHAHJO-KOTIRO
THANO BULA KHAN
ALLAHDINO
KARACHI

LAND ABOVE 4000 FT

SUTKAGEN-DOR

PAKISTAN

AREA OF MAP

DESALPAR

ARABIAN SEA

HALAR
RANGPUR
LOTHAL
AMARA
KINNARKHEDA
MEHGAM
R. NARBADA
TELOD
BHAGATRA
R. TAPTI
SOMNATH
GULF OF CAMBAY

2. Indus Civilization Sites

short and life itself was hard, 'religion' centred almost entirely on fertility and the powers that controlled fertility. Strange though it may seem, despite all that has happened in the meantime, *popular* Hinduism is not so very different — perhaps because for most people, life in India is much the same as it always has been.

The Indus Culture

Archaeology (the rediscovery of long-buried worlds) can be an exciting business. One of the most exciting discoveries which has been made this century is that of the ancient civilization of India, called, after the great river of the north-west, the Indus Culture (or the Indus Valley Civilization). It was all the more remarkable because no one suspected it

15

was there. Scholars thought that the real history of India began with the coming of the Aryan invaders in about 1500 B.C. (we shall talk about these in the next chapter), and that the Aryans simply met and conquered bands of savages, who could have contributed nothing to the future of India. But they were wrong.

We now know that a brilliant and powerful civilization existed in India long before the Aryans came. It extended over about half a million square miles. Archaeologists have dug up a number of cities and towns, two of which are of great importance. Their names are Mohenjo-daro and Harappa. Mohenjo-daro in particular has given us a great deal of valuable information about the earliest Indian writing (which unfortunately no one is as yet able to read), about commerce, about town planning and about religion. We cannot be sure that we know everything about these first Hindus, the people of the Indus Culture; but there are some things about them which are worth pointing out.

In many of the houses, there have been found figures which seem to represent mother-goddesses, that is, symbols of the earth in human form. Often these figures are smoke-stained, as though they had stood for years with a little lamp burning in front of them. Similar figures are still found in Indian villages today. Why? Because the earth is still regarded as the great mother — Mother India — and the burning of the lamp, together with the making of small offerings of, for instance, flowers and fruit, is an act of respect and reverence to the giver of all things. Another symbol found in the Indus Culture is the *swastika* (the word means 'Bringer of good fortune'), representing the sun.

The people of Mohenjo-daro were great traders. In their trading they made use of small seals, about an inch and a half square (rather like an old-fashioned signet ring). Many of these have been found. Some have pictures of animals on them: the cow is common, and so is the bull, and there are elephants, tigers and rhinoceros. Others carry pictures of what can only be gods and goddesses. One in particular has a figure which seems to represent the god Shiva, 'the gracious one'. He has horns and three faces, he is surrounded by animals, and he is seated in the position of a Yogin. Shiva is still today called 'Lord of Beasts' and 'Prince of Yogis', as well as being a great giver of fertility. It seems that here we have an example of a god being worshipped in more or less the same way for more than twice the length of the total history of Christianity. A modern image of Shiva is on p. 17.

One of the most interesting buildings found on an Indus site, at Mohenjo-daro, has been called by archaeologists 'The Great Bath'. This was

3. Shiva Nataraja, Lord of the Dance

not a swimming bath, but a bath for ritual washing, in which people prepared themselves for worship by symbolically washing away their sins and impurities. Again it seems that we are looking at the beginnings of an unbroken tradition. The larger temples in India still have such baths today, sometimes much bigger baths than this one, and many ceremonies are carried out in their waters. In one corner you may see a wedding party, accompanied by a little group of musicians, completing a marriage ceremony with a sprinkling of holy water. In another, you might see a man washing himself all over in preparation for entering a nearby temple; seasons of pilgrimage would see the steps crowded, while the surrounding shops and shrines would all be doing excellent business. Of course we do not know exactly how the Mohenjo-daro bath was used, but we are probably not wrong in imagining similar scenes there.

The important thing to bear in mind in this first look at Hinduism is that it has some right to be called the oldest religion in the world, and that it has from the first been intimately connected with the land and life of India. We shall see that *tradition* is very important in Hinduism — tradition in things done and tradition in things believed. We shall also see that the traditional way of doing things does not always fit in with a modern way of life. If traditions and beliefs are suitable for a nation of farmers, that does not necessarily mean that they are going to be suitable for an industrial nation.

Hinduism does not only rest on traditional ways of doing things, however. It has holy scriptures which can be referred to for authority and guidance. How these scriptures came to be written we shall consider in the next chapter.

2
SCRIPTURES AND GODS

All the great religions have holy scriptures, usually books which are connected in some way either with the founder of the religion in question or with the first community of believers. The Christian Bible and the Muslim Qur'an are scriptures of this type; from them the reader may learn something of the founder and his original teachings. But we have seen that Hinduism has no founder, though it does have many men (and some women) who are regarded as saints, and whose writings are therefore looked upon as holy scripture.

This is not to say however, that the Hindu regards all scriptures as equally holy. In practice, he divides scriptures up into two categories.

1. Revelation (in Sanskrit* *shruti*): scriptures which are believed by the faithful to be of divine origin, without any real human intervention.
2. Tradition (in Sanskrit *smriti*): scriptures which are recognised to have human authors, but which are nevertheless important and authoritative, though not as authoritative as *shruti*.

We shall look at each of these in turn.

Revealed Scripture

In the last chapter, we saw something of the first civilization of India, the Indus Culture or the Indus Valley Civilization. Archaeologists tell us that it appears to have been destroyed in about 1750 B.C. by bands of nomadic horsemen coming across the mountains from the north-west. These nomads called themselves 'nobles', or *Aryans*. After overcoming the remnants of the Indus Valley Civilization (which in any case seems to have been in decline) they settled in that part of India which is now the Punjab (see map) and gradually extended their influence over the greater part of the north of India.

* The sacred language of Hinduism.

The religion of the Aryans was unlike that of the Indus Valley in that it was concerned more with the sky than with the earth. Its gods and goddesses were personifications of things like the sky itself (the greatest of the gods), the storm, the sun and the dawn. The invaders brought with them a tradition of singing hymns to their gods; not congregational singing as in a modern church, but part of the action of the priests as they offered sacrifices. At first, these hymns were not written down, in fact, they were put into writing only in modern times. But it is these hymns that form the foundation of Hindu revealed scripture. Their authors are, of course, unknown; but they have been so important in the history of Hinduism that they are believed to have come direct from God.

These hymns are divided into four groups:

1. The Rig Veda (the knowledge (= *veda*) of the praises).
2. The Sama Veda (the knowledge of the chants).
3. The Yajur Veda (the knowledge of the sacrificial ritual).
4. The Atharva Veda (the meaning of the word *atharva* is uncertain).

Of the four, the *Rig Veda* is by far the most important; it contains over a thousand hymns, usually addressed to individual gods or goddesses. Here are some examples:

A Hymn to Agni, God of Fire

I praise Agni, the chosen priest, god, minister of sacrifice,
The hotar [sacrificial priest], most generous giver of wealth.
Worthy is Agni to be praised by living as by ancient seers:
He shall bring the gods here to us.
Through Agni man obtains wealth, yea, plenty, growing day by day,
Most rich in heroes, glorious.
Agni, the perfect sacrifice which you encompass about
Truly goes to the gods . . .

A Hymn to Ushas, Goddess of the Dawn

In all ages has the goddess Dawn shone, and shows her light today,
endowed with riches.
So will she shine on coming days; immortal and undecaying, she
moves on in her own strength.
In the sky's borders has she shone in splendour: the goddess has
cast off the veil of darkness.
Dawn approaches in her magnificent chariot, awakening the world
with purple horses . . .

A Hymn to Varuna, God of the Sky

If we have sinned against the man who loves us, have ever wronged
a brother, friend, or comrade,
The neighbour ever with us, or a stranger, O Varuna, remove from
us the trespass.
If we, as gamblers cheat at play, have cheated, done wrong un-
wittingly or sinned deliberately,
Cast all these sins away like loosened fetters, and, Varuna, let us
be your own beloved.

A Daily Prayer from the Rig Veda

We meditate on the loving light of the god, Savitri [a sun-god]
May it stimulate our thoughts!

These hymns, and others like them, were chanted by priests in the
process of offering sacrifice to the gods; and to each of the four collections
of hymns (actually five, for the *Yajur Veda* was divided into two) was
added a commentary, dealing with the words of the hymns themselves and
with details of the action of the sacrifice.

These commentaries are called *Brahmanas* (*brahman* = word), and are
of interest only to specialists. Many of them are of great length and very
complicated.

In time, to each of the commentaries was further added another book,
answering the question 'What is it all about?' These books are called
Upanishads, meaning roughly 'sitting down together', or 'discussions'.
Again, they can be very difficult to understand. We shall have a closer look
at them in the next chapter, because they are very important for the future
of Hindu beliefs.

All these together, *Vedas* plus *Brahmanas* plus *Upanishads*, are the
Hindus' most holy scriptures, and it is one test of an orthodox Hindu
whether or not he believes in the divine inspiration of these scriptures.
Together they are called the *Veda* (knowledge).

Traditional Scripture

Most Hindus do not read the *Veda*, or at least only very small parts of it.
(How many Christians have read, and are familiar with, the *whole* of the
Bible or even such books as Deuteronomy or Numbers?) What they *do*
read, or have read to them, will depend to some extent·on the sect to which
they belong or the part of India in which they live and the language they
speak. Almost any religious writing can be regarded as sacred, that is, as

21

belonging to the category of tradition. And traditional scriptures have been accumulating over a period of more than 2500 years, so there are quite a lot of them!

There are commentaries on the *Veda* by famous philosophers; there are books of law and devotional writings; there are poems and dramas; and perhaps most important of all (at least to the common people) there are the great epics, the *Ramayana* and the *Mahabharata*, which are part history and part legend, not unlike the Greek *Iliad* and *Odyssey*. We shall be looking at them a little more closely in chapter four, but there are one or two facts about them which may be mentioned now.

The Ramayana tells the story of the god Rama and his wife Sita, set against the background of a great war. It was composed (at least in part) by the poet Valmiki, between 500 B.C. and the beginning of the Christian era.

The Mahabharata, or great Indian epic (*Bharat* = India; *maha* = great), is larger and a little more recent. Again it is set against the background of a war between two princely families, and one of its central characters is the god Krishna, who acts as the charioteer of prince Arjuna in the greatest of the battles. The episode in which this battle is described, and in which Krishna teaches Arjuna about the problems of war and life, is now the most popular of Hindu scriptures, and is called the *Bhagavad Gita*, or song of the adorable one (*gita* = song; *bhagavad* = adorable), the 'adorable one' being Krishna.

It was once said of the *Mahabharata* that 'What is not in it, is nowhere.' The two epics together have been said to contain 'India's message to man', and a recent editor of a pocket edition of the two wrote:

> I appeal particularly to the young men in schools and colleges to read these books. There is not a page in them but after reading you will emerge with greater courage, stronger will and purer mind. They are not just story books, although they are very good in that way too. They are the records of the mind and spirit of our forefathers . . . Let us keep ever in our minds the fact that it is the *Ramayana* and the *Mahabharata* that bind our vast numbers together as one people, despite caste, space and language that seemingly divide them.

Another class of traditional scripture which may be mentioned here is the *Purana* (antiquity). There are eighteen principal *Puranas* and a large number of lesser ones. Each is devoted to a description of the character and deeds of one of the great gods, but there is a great deal of legendary material added, including, for example, accounts of the creation of the world.

4. Hindu Temple in Madras showing intricate carvings

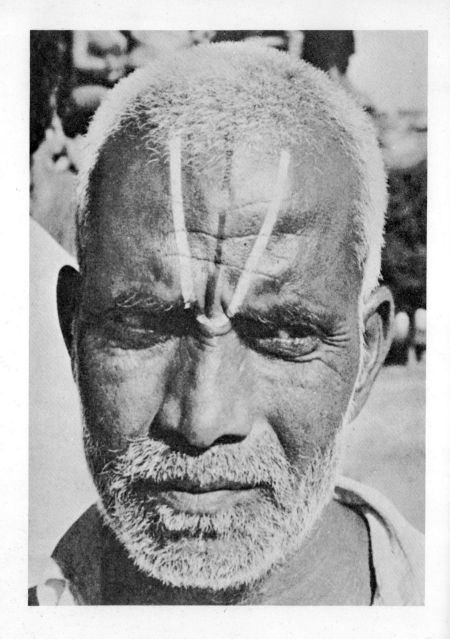

5. A worshipper of Vishnu, wearing the mark of the Shri-Vaishnava Sect on his forehead

The scriptures we have mentioned by no means exhaust the list of Hindu holy books, and it is doubtful whether any one person could ever hope to master more than a fraction of them.

The Great Gods

The Westerner, reading a Hindu scripture for the first time, is bewildered by the great number of names of gods and goddesses that appear in its pages. At first there appear to have been thirty-three great gods, though as time went on, the list grew into the thousands; but from the time of the *Rig Veda* on, thinkers were beginning to say that there was really only one, as this verse shows:

It is called Indra, Mitra, Varuna and Agni
And also Garutman the lovely-winged in heaven.
The real is one, though known by different names:
It is called now Agni, now Yama, now Matarishvan.

Most Hindus today would insist that this is so: that, in simple language, there is only one God, though he may have as many names as he has characteristics, and though 'he' may be both god and goddess. He is everywhere, and in all things, all animals and all men (this is called *pantheism*), though he may choose to show himself in some places and situations more than in others, and may wish to be worshipped under certain names.

Present-day Hindus tend to worship under one of two names, and much of Hinduism therefore falls into two classes, or sects. These names are Vishnu and Shiva. These are not the only classes, or the only sects, but they are by far the largest and most important. Each has its own scriptures; many of those we have so far mentioned were written by worshippers of Vishnu, but there is also an extensive literature about Shiva, much of which is better known in the south than in the north of India, and is written in Tamil, not Sanskrit.

Historically, the difference between the two is that while Vishnu was originally a Vedic god of the sky, Shiva was originally an Indus god of the earth. But this is of little significance today. Each has a 'family' (not to be taken literally, of course): for instance, the goddess Parvati is looked upon as the wife of Shiva and Lakshmi as the wife of Vishnu; the elephant-headed god of wisdom Ganesha is associated with Shiva, while the monkey-god Hanuman is associated with Vishnu. Each has appropriate animals and birds (the peacock, the cobra and the bull in the case of Shiva); and the devotees of each wear distinctive markings. See the

25

6. Nandi, the White Bull on which the God Shiva is believed to ride

illustration on p. 24.

Peculiar to the worship of Vishnu is, however, the belief in incarnation, as the god comes to earth in some human or animal form (the Sanskrit word is *avatara*). The greatest incarnations of Vishnu are Rama and Krishna. In the *Bhagavad Gita*, Krishna explains how he came to be 'made man':

> For whenever the law of righteousness
> Withers away, and lawlessness
>   Raises its head,
> Then do I generate Myself on earth.
> For the protection of the good,
> For the destruction of evildoers,
> For the setting up of righteousness,
> I come into being, age after age.

In fact it is the Lord Krishna, the lover of mankind, the restorer of justice and the teacher of Arjuna, who is the most 'popular' of all Hindu gods, who inspires the greatest devotion and who seems the most human, as well as the most divine of deities.

For those men who meditate upon Me, no other
  thought in mind,
Who do me honour, ever persevere,
I bring attainment
And possession of what has been attained.

However evil a man's livelihood may be,
Let him but worship Me with love and serve no other,
Then shall he be reckoned among the good indeed,
For his resolve is right.

Right soon will his self be filled with righteousness
And win eternal rest.
Arjuna, of this be sure:
None who pays me worship of loyalty and love is
  ever lost.

3

THE SEARCH FOR KNOWLEDGE

In any religion there tends to be a difference between the beliefs and practices of the common people, and those of the few who devote themselves altogether to thinking about the problems of life. In Hinduism there is a particularly deep tradition of philosophical thought, which we in the west do not find easy to understand, but which has played such a large part in the history of India that we cannot avoid looking at it at this point. India has always admired the holy man, that is, the man who has left the world in order to devote himself to the things of the spirit. Hindu tradition speaks of the four stages of life, which are:

1. The student, who devotes himself to the study of the *Veda* under the guidance of a personal teacher, or *guru*.
2. The householder, who marries and brings up a family.
3. The hermit, who takes his wife with him into the forest and lives a life of study, meditation and prayer.
4. The holy man, or *sannyasin*, who abandons even his wife and family in order to seek for truth.

In fact, very few Hindus pass beyond these first two stages, or have any desire to do so; but the ideal of complete dedication to the search for knowledge about life, about the world and about reality has always been a powerful one. Even in the modern world, where it is impossible for a man to leave his responsibilities, the average Hindu will regard the *sannyasin* with reverence.

What does this search for knowledge involve? In order to find the answer, we must go back to chapter two (p. 21), to those scriptures which are called *Upanishads*. We saw that the meaning of the word *Upanishad* was something like 'sitting down together' or 'discussion', and they give us the substance of what the best teachers taught, almost 2500 years ago, about life and its problems.

There are over a hundred of these *Upanishads*, and some of them are very long and complicated. Traditionally, about a dozen have been looked upon as authoritative. They do not all teach the same things (and this gives rise to further problems, as we shall see), but their general teaching may be summed up in a prayer which we find in the *Brihadaranyaka Upanishad*:

> From the unreal lead me to the real!
> From darkness lead me to the light!
> From death lead me to immortality!

They teach, then, the way to reality, light and immortality: these three are in fact one and the same.

At the same time, they teach the way out of unreality, darkness and mortality: again, these are one and the same. But what are they? Before we can answer this question, we must look at three basic beliefs and one practice shared by practically all Hindus.

The Belief in Transmigration

Hindus (and Buddhists, and some people in the west) believe that all human beings live not one life, but a series of lives on earth. The human soul remains the same, but passes through any number of bodies, which it wears out, much as old clothes are worn out. A verse from the *Bhagavad Gita* (see above, p. 22) illustrates this.

> As a man casts off his worn-out clothes
> And takes on other new ones in their place,
> So does the embodied soul cast off his worn-out bodies
>   And enters others new.

Except in very unusual cases, though, the individual has no memory of his or her former lives. This is called the transmigration of souls or reincarnation (that is, becoming man again).

The Belief in Karma

Some men are rich, others poor; some are healthy, others sick; some are happy, others suffer. Traditionally, Hindus have explained this by saying that in every life, a man or woman does good or bad things. Another way of putting it is that he or she collects good or bad *karma* (*karma* = works or deeds) and this is what decides the kind of life that will be lived next time round. Suffering can be explained as being the result of a bad *karma* in a man's last life.

The Belief in Maya

To the westerner, the world is very real, and success is measured by the individual's capacity for living happily and profitably in the world. In the east, on the other hand, the world has seldom or never occupied this unquestioned place in man's interest. The key to the traditional Hindu view is provided by the word *maya*.

Maya is generally taken to mean 'illusion', and some Hindu writings suggest that the world is not real, but only appears to be real because of *maya*. *Maya* is like a veil drawn between man and reality, which makes things seem different from what they are. So while the world is changing, reality does not change. Put it another way, the world is real enough from the human point of view, but from the divine point of view, it is not. Transmigration and *karma* belong to the 'unreal' world of *maya*.

These are unusual ideas from our point of view, but they form the starting point of Hindu philosophy. Now we must try to sum up what the *Upanishads* teach that man must do about this life.

In a word, he must escape from it.

He does this by means of knowledge. He must know that his soul, or self (the Sanskrit word is *atman*) is the only real part of him. And he must know that the universe, too, has a soul, called *Brahman*. He must reject the world as he sees and experiences it, and turn entirely to the inner world of the self. When he sees through the deception of *maya* and the unreality of the world, he is set free from rebirth. This release, escape or salvation is called *moksha*. In it, he recognizes that his own soul is identical with the soul of the universe. *Brahman* is *atman*.

This is what one of the *Upanishads* says about the self: that it is 'smaller than a grain of rice . . . greater than the earth . . . This my self within the heart is that Brahman. When I depart from hence I shall merge into it. He who believes this will never doubt.' And again: 'This finest essence – the whole universe has it as its self: that is the real: That is the self: That *you* are . . .'

This is not teaching for everyone, but for a chosen few. As the *Katha Upanishad* says,

Many there are who never come to hear of him (the self),
Many, though hearing of him, know him not:

7. A Sannyasin (holy man) practising Yoga

> Blessed the man who, skilled therein, proclaims him,
>   grasps him;
> Blessed the man who learns from one so skilled and
>   knows him!

The complications of the teaching of the *Upanishads* led in time to the formation of a number of schools of thought. Some of these were counted orthodox, because those who followed them believed in the divine authority of the *Vedas*; others were reckoned unorthodox, because their followers did not accept the *Vedas*.

The Practice of Yoga

Everyone knows about the postures and the breath-control exercises of Yoga. But Yoga is not only a system of difficult gymnastics, although physical discipline plays a part in it; it is a means of releasing the soul from the body, and thus reaching salvation.

Here is another quotation from the *Gita*, in which the ideal of Yoga is put very clearly (a Yogin is one who practises Yoga):

31

Let the Yogin ever integrate himself
Standing in a place apart,
Alone, his thoughts and self restrained,
Devoid of (earthly) hope, nothing possessing.

Let him for himself set up
A steady seat in a clean place,
Neither too high nor yet too low,
With cloth or hides or grass bestrewn.

There let him sit and make his mind a single point;
Let him restrain the motions of his thought and senses,
And engage in spiritual exercises (yoga)
To purify the self.

Remaining still, let him keep body, head and neck
In a straight line, unmoving;
Let him fix his gaze on the tip of his own nose,
Not looking round about him.

There let him sit, his self all stilled,
His fear all gone, firm in his vow of chastity,
His mind controlled, his thoughts on Me (Krishna = God)
Integrated, (yet) intent on Me.

As a method of physical and spiritual discipline, Yoga has been practised throughout India for centuries, and more and more people outside India are coming to learn its physical benefits. But the Hindu would say that it is only a means to an end — the same end that we have been speaking about in this chapter, of the quest for knowledge.

4
STORIES OF GODS AND MEN

The average Hindu, though he may respect and reverence the holy man and the philosopher, is not greatly concerned with that side of Hinduism we were talking about in the last chapter. It is true that he believes that every man ought to be seeking for salvation (*moksha*), but he believes that he has many lives on earth in which to find it. His way of salvation is much simpler than that of the philosopher. It turns not around *knowledge* but around good works and devotion to God.

By good works (*karma*) Hinduism traditionally means observing the rules of the *caste* into which the individual is born, and in which he is brought up. But the service of humanity is also important, particularly in modern Hinduism.

Devotion (*bhakti*) may be shown to God in any form, and under any name. Hinduism has a rich and beautiful store of devotional hymns and other writings, coming from many parts of India and many periods. Here is just one short example, a hymn by Tukaram (1607–1649):

No deeds I've done nor thoughts I've thought;
Save as thy servant, I am naught.

Guard me, O God, and O, control
The tumult of my restless soul.

Ah, do not, do not cast on me
The guilt of mine iniquity.

My countless sins, I, Tuka, say,
Upon thy loving heart I lay.

Popular Hinduism, in the sense of the Hinduism of the common people of India, is not easily described, because it varies a good deal between different parts of the country. There is, however, one feature in particular that must be noted, and that is its use of some of the holy scriptures that were mentioned in chapter two. These are the great epics, the *Ramayana* and the *Mahabharata* (including the *Bhagavad Gita*), and the *Puranas*. (See above, p. 22.)

It is on the stories contained in these huge books that the ordinary Hindu bases his daily life. They tell of kings, queens, princes, princesses, holy men, gods, demons and ordinary men and women, and they are taken as parables, showing the way in which people ought to behave. Perhaps the villager cannot read them for himself (many Indian villagers are still illiterate), but he will have them read to him by a teacher (pandit).

The Role of the Pandit

In the Indian village, the pandit is an important person. As well as looking after the village temple, he is a deep student of holy scripture. He began learning the *Vedas* when he was only seven years old, and knows the greater part of them by heart. He also knows by heart most of the 24,000 stanzas of the *Ramayana*, the 100,000 stanzas of the *Mahabharata* and the 18,000 stanzas of the *Bhagavata Purana*. As a Brahmin (a member of the highest caste) his head is shaved, except for a small tuft on top, and he wears a sacred thread across his left shoulder and a silver ring. He bathes twice daily at the village pool, and prays three times every day, facing east or west according to the time. He believes that the *Vedas* were created out of the breath of God, and contain everything that man needs for salvation. The stories that he tells to the people in the evening are important, but not as important to him as the *Vedas*, and he will say that 'No one can understand the significance of any story in our mythology unless he is deeply versed in the *Vedas*.' Yet he will suit his story-telling to the needs and the education of the people, giving them patterns of goodness and truth and devotion and honour which they will then try to follow. Of course, the people will also enjoy the stories as good stories; but they come to the pandit to be taught, and not just to be entertained. They may hear the same stories over and over again, but they never get tired of them, because they help them to understand the meaning of life.

The Bhagavad Gita

Of all the countless stories that go to make up popular Hindu scripture, the one with the widest appeal is certainly the *Bhagavad Gita* (part of the

Mahabharata, see above, p. 22), and there is some point in saying that anyone who understands the *Gita* understands Hinduism, for although it is part of the heritage of story that we are thinking about in this chapter, it contains profound spiritual teaching, too.

The action of the *Gita* takes place on a battlefield, where two opposing armies are drawn up, ready to fight. On one side there is the army of the five sons of Pandu; on the other, the army of the sons of Dhritarashtra, Pandu's brother. The point here is that the two armies are related to each other as part of the same family.

One of the sons of Pandu is Prince Arjuna, whose charioteer is Krishna. Arjuna drives into an observation position, ready to start the battle, and is then suddenly struck by the fact that he is about to kill his relatives. He tells Krishna that he simply cannot do it:

> Krishna, when these mine own folk I see
> Standing before me, spoiling for the fight,
> My limbs give way . . .
> Should I strike down in battle mine own folk
>   No good therein see I . . .
> They are our venerable teachers, fathers, sons,
> They too our grandsires, uncles,
> Fathers-in-law, grandsons,
> Brothers-in-law, kinsmen all.

He cannot do it, because he is committing a crime against the family.

On the other hand, he is a warrior, a member of the *Kshatriya* class (see below, p. 48) and, as such, it is his sacred duty to fight. Krishna (who is really the god Vishnu in human form) reminds him of this, and tells him that in any case, he will not hurt the souls of his relatives by killing them. All men, he says, put on bodies as they put on clothes. The soul, or self, passes from one to another, but cannot itself be hurt.

> As a man casts off his worn-out clothes
> And takes on other new ones in their place,
> So does the embodied soul cast off his worn-out bodies
>   And enters others new.

Therefore Arjuna ought to do his duty and fight.

But Arjuna is not satisfied, even when Krishna tells him that if he runs away from the battle, people will call him a coward. And so Krishna begins to teach him about the real meaning and purpose of life. The lesson is a long and often complicated one, but its main points are:

1. You must do the duty prescribed for your class.

> Better one's own duty to perform, though void of merit,
>   Than to do another's well;
> Better to die within the sphere of one's own duty;
>   Perilous is the duty of other men.

2. You must never worry about results.

Wisdom consists in doing one's duty without thought of reward. The most dangerous thing for man is desire; and desire must be brought under control, by yoga (above, p. 31). Otherwise, he is a slave of desire.

> The integrated man, renouncing the fruit of works,
>   Gains an abiding peace:
> The man not integrated, whose works are prompted by desire,
>   Holds fast to fruits and thus remains enslaved.

Other important teachings of the *Gita* have to do with God. The *Gita* teaches that God can take human form at any time, and has often done so. (This is rather different from the Christian belief that God became man only once.) Krishna says:

> For whenever the law of righteousness
> Withers away, and lawlessness
>   Raises its head,
> Then do I generate myself on earth.
> For the protection of the good,
> For the destruction of evildoers,
> For the setting up of righteousness,
> I come into being, age after age.

God in *Gita* is a loving God, prepared to accept the man or woman who shows devotion (*bhakti*, above, p. 33). Krishna tells Arjuna that 'those who sacrifice to me shall come to me', and continues:

> Be it a leaf, or flower, or fruit, or water
> That a zealous soul may offer with love's devotion
>   (*bhakti*)
>   That do I willingly accept,
> For it was love (*bhakti*) that made the offering.

Even worshippers of other gods than Krishna, who do not know Krishna, are accepted by him if their intention is pure:

36

Yet even those who worship other gods with love
And sacrifice to them, full filled with faith,
    Do really worship me . . .
For it is I who of all acts of sacrifice
    Am recipient and lord . . .

There is no teaching that is more characteristic of Hinduism than this: that all 'religions' are equal in the sight of God. Krishna then shows Arjuna his true supernatural nature which frightens him almost out of his wits. Soon he returns to his familiar form as a charioteer, and the *Gita* ends with more teaching, perhaps summed up in the words:

Turn to me, thine only refuge,
For I will deliver thee
From all evils; have no care.

Arjuna's last comment is:
With doubts dispelled I stand
Ready to do thy bidding.

What does the *Gita* mean to the Hindu? The philosopher Shankara wrote, in the 7th century:

When doubts haunt me, when disappointment stares me in the face and when I see not one ray of light on the horizon, I turn to the *Gita*, and find a verse to comfort me, and I immediately begin to smile in the midst of overwhelming sorrow. My life is full of external tragedies, and if they have not left any visible and indelible effects on me I owe it to the teachings of that great work, the *Gita*.

Mahatma Gandhi referred to it as his 'infallible guide of conduct'. Nehru, though not himself very religious, said that there was something in the *Gita* 'which seems to be capable of being constantly renewed, which does not become out of date with the passing of time'. Another commentator (M. A. Kamath) calls it 'an inexhaustible treasure-house of spiritual wisdom'.

Finally, we have these words, by Gandhi's disciple Vinoba Bhave:

Where the heart is touched, there is no room for argument. Leaving logic behind, I beat the twin wings of faith and practice and, to the best of my ability, fly up into the heavens of the *Gita*. I live and move in the atmosphere of the *Gita*. The *Gita* is my life's breath. To vary the image, I swim in the sea of the *Gita* when I speak of it; but when I am alone, I dive to the depths of this ocean of nectar and there rest at ease.

5

WORSHIP IN HOME AND TEMPLE

To the Christian, the worship of God is something which people do together. Although private prayer, whether at home or in church, is important, most Christians regard going to church to receive holy communion, to sing hymns, to pray and listen to sermons *together* as the high point of their week.

For the Hindu, this is not so. When a Hindu offers worship (*puja*) to God, he does so on his own. And even when there are large numbers of individuals worshipping at the same time in the same place (as on the great festivals), they do so as individuals. The main reason for this is that Hindus believe that it is necessary to have a right attitude of mind when worshipping, and that salvation (*moksha*, see above, p. 30) is something to be found by each person separately. So while some Christians would say that one has to attend church services in order to be a Christian in the proper sense, Hindus would make no such claim. The Hindu may attend the temple or not, as he pleases. His status as a Hindu does not depend on this.

The temple is not the only place in which the Hindu worships. He does so at home, too, often in a room or part of a room set aside for that purpose. But before we look more closely at what the Hindu does when worshipping in his home or the temple, a few words must be said about ministers, i.e., those responsible in a special way for Hindu worship.

The Temple Priest (pujari)

Every temple has its own staff of priests, their numbers varying with the size of the temple. Some are well educated; many are not. Most (though

8. Image of Shri Ramakrishna in the meditation hall of Ramakrishna Mission, Bombay

9. Bathing Ghats on the River Ganges at Hardwar

not all) are Brahmins (members of the priestly class). They are responsible for the care of the building, and for the regular round of ceremonies connected with the image of the God.

The Household Priest

Since the householder may not have the time or the knowledge to carry out all the duties prescribed for him as a Hindu, he may hire a priest to visit his home at regular intervals to help him carry out the ceremonies properly.

The Guru

It is held by many Hindus that spiritual progress is to be gained only by direct personal teaching from someone of high spiritual status. Such a counsellor or teacher is called a *guru* or an *acharya*.

The Pandit

A learned man, who decides questions of conduct and offers instruction to all who desire it. (See above, p. 34.)

The Swami

A *swami* is a monk, i.e., a senior member of a Hindu religious order, and therefore subject to vows of poverty, chastity and obedience. He dresses in a saffron-yellow robe, and very often has a teaching ministry, either by writing or preaching.

In general, no act of worship can be undertaken without purification of oneself, the place where one worships, and the various objects used. As far as the individual is concerned, purity is both external and internal. External purity is gained by washing in a sacred river or pool (wherever possible), or some other source; internal purity is gained by study and meditation, and often by yoga (see above, p. 31).

Worship in the Home

In the home of the devout Hindu there is a *puja* room, which contains images of the god or gods in which he worships the one Reality. These may be small statues, often of great beauty, or, in the case of poorer families, just pictures. As well as pictures of Hindu gods and goddesses, it is not uncommon to see pictures of modern saints, such as Mahatma Gandhi, or even (to the Christian's surprise) a picture of Jesus. The *puja* room may also contain various symbols of the family's chosen deity

Worship begins before dawn, with an act of dedication for the coming day; then, after a bath, morning worship is performed, which includes the *Gayatri* (the invocation of the sun, see p. 21) repeated a number of times. Midday worship may take place any time after sunrise, and includes offerings to God of flowers, incense and food. The round of daily devotion ends with evening worship, after which the image of god is retired for the night, and the evening meal is taken.

In addition, the orthodox Hindu performs regular rites of remembrance and reverence (called *shraddha*) for his deceased relatives; and there are important ceremonies to be held on the birth of a child, initiation of a young person as an adult member of the caste and family, marriage and death. The marriage ceremony in particular is both beautiful and profound. It takes place in the home, although it may be concluded at a temple or temple pool.

First the father of the bride 'worships' the bridegroom, using the same gestures as those which he would use in *puja* before a god. Then an act of consecration is performed by the women of the bride's family. The bride is 'given away' by her parents, at which time the genealogy of both bride and groom is recited. When the groom accepts the hand of the bride, a fire offering is made, followed by the Seven Steps, in which the couple go round the fire seven times. The ceremony concludes with an act in which the bride acknowledges the groom 'as of herself in body and mind', and with prayers for good fortune and for peace. Usually there is then a celebration for family and friends, which may represent a family's accumulated savings of years.

Most Hindu marriages are still arranged by the parents or other relatives of the couple, particular attention being paid to the horoscopes of the young people and (usually) to caste. Newspapers have matrimonial columns, from which this is a typical entry:

WANTED Vadama Non-Bharadwaja [caste] bridegroom for girl, 28, Sevvai Thosham, Secondary Grade trained, well-versed in domestic duties. Also bride for her brother, 31, employed in State Bank, Madurai, drawing Rs. 450. Mutual alliance alone considered. Reply with horoscope and full particulars to Box No. 6731, c/o *The Hindu*.

Funerals also fall within the category of worship in the home, although the essential ceremonies are carried out partly there, and partly in a public place. If a person has died in a house, a group of drummers will often be hired to beat their drums as the body is prepared for cremation. Their original function was almost certainly to drive away the ghost and other evil spirits from the house, although this is not necessarily believed today.

10. Funeral pyre on the river bank

If possible, the dying person is taken to die on a river bank, and the corpse is then cremated, the torch being applied by the eldest son, or the nearest male relative. There was once a custom by which a man's widow would burn herself to death on her husband's funeral pyre in order to pass with him into the life beyond, but this custom (called *sati*) was abolished by law over a century ago.

It is believed that the soul of the dead person passes into a heaven or hell, after which he (or she) is in time reborn (see above, p. 29, below, p. 49).

Worship in the Temple

India is a land of temples, ranging from the huge cathedral temples of the popular centres to the tiny shrines which are found in every village and at intervals along every road. It must be remembered that a temple is not a church: that is, it is not a place for congregational worship, but the dwelling place of a god or goddess, to which the individual worshipper comes to pay respects.

There may seem to be a contradiction between the idea that God is everywhere and in all things, and the notion of a god having a temple as his home. The latter statement is to be understood symbolically. In Hindu belief, the Supreme Being may manifest himself in many forms and in many places, and be known by many names. Thus if he chooses a particular form in a particular place, this is his own choice, for which man may be grateful, since it makes worship easier. Images of gods or goddesses are usually understood as aids to worship. As one modern Hindu writer, Vinoba Bhave, has put it, the worship of an image is 'the art of embracing the whole universe in a little object'.

In the temple, the main image is in a central shrine (possibly, in the larger temples, surrounded by lesser shrines), and elaborate care is taken of the image, since God manifests himself in it.

The temple day begins with the awakening of the god, accompanied by music, after which the image is bathed, fed, and decorated with sandal paste. During the day the god has to be fed frequently (52 times during the day at one of the largest temples, that at Puri) and has to have his period of rest, when no worshipper may approach. And at the end of the day, he is put to rest with further ceremonies. During the greater part of the day there is a constant stream of visitors, saying prayers, listening to discourses, offering gifts of flowers, food, garlands, ornaments, for which privilege they pay a small fee to the attendant priests. These are all signs of devotion to the god or goddess whose home the temple is; they are also sources of

11. On a pilgrimage

merit to the worshipper.

Pilgrimages

Special merit is obtained by going on pilgrimage to some particularly holy place, either a temple or a place hallowed by association with some deity. One writer has described the reason for pilgrimages in these words.

Pilgrimages to the shrines of India are undertaken for the completion of vows, for the appeasing of the deity in times of misfortunes, to gain prosperity and good fortune, and as simple acts of devotion to the Lord. Toward the end of life when people are expected to be more godly minded, when the pettiness of earthly life seems to fade away, they are more inclined to go on pilgrimages to sacred spots. After the death of a parent, the son longs for the opportunity to visit Gaya, Banaras, and Allahabad to perform there the ceremonial rites for his father and mother. And at the time of the great festivals, when thousands of pilgrims gather to witness the ceremonies, there is a strong urge for the devout Hindu to join them.

6
WHAT IS A HINDU?

We began by looking at the connection between Hinduism and India, and by saying that Hinduism is the traditional religion of India in one or another form. It follows from this that a Hindu is one who observes this traditional religion in some way. But we have also seen that there are very many different expressions of Hinduism, as indeed there are of any religion. What we must now ask is whether there are any beliefs which *all* Hindus hold in common.

Probably there are not. If we were to look closely enough at the religion of India, we should find exceptions to any and every rule. As in any religion, there are orthodox believers, who take their beliefs and practices very seriously indeed, while others are more liberal. Different schools, sects and groups do not hold to all things equally. Nevertheless there are five main areas of belief and practice in which the majority of Hindus have a great deal in common. To us, they may not all appear to be equally religious; but we must remember that the hard-and-fast distinction between religious and secular attitudes to which we are accustomed, seldom applies in India.

Class and Caste

The word 'caste' came originally from a Portuguese word meaning 'pure'; the Indian words are *varna*, 'colour' and *jati*, 'birth'. Traditionally, Indian society has been divided into a large number of castes, or social groups. They are rather like enlarged families, although they have some features in common with trades union — that is, all their members have normally followed a certain occupation or trade.

Originally, there were four main class groups:
1. *Brahmanas*, or *Brahmins*: priests.
2. *Kshatriyas*: rulers and warriors.
3. *Vaishyas*: tradesmen, artisans and farmers. Common people
4. *Shudras*: labourers.

A fifth group comprised the so-called outcastes, or people who did not belong to any of these four categories.

A famous passage from the *Rig Veda* describes the supernatural origin of the classes. The hymn in which it occurs is a hymn of creation, and speaks of the creation of the world from the body of a giant — primal man.

> When they divided [primal] man,
> Into how many parts did they divide him?
> What was his mouth? What his arms?
> What are his thighs called? What his feet?
>
> The Brahman was his mouth,
> The arms were made the Prince (*Kshatriya*),
> His thighs the common people (*Vaishya*),
> And from his feet the serf (*Shudra*) was born.

In the course of time, the priestly class came to occupy a position of superiority over again all other castes. The Laws of Manu express it like this:

> Of created beings the most excellent are said to be those that are animated; of the animated, those that subsist by intelligence; of the intelligent, mankind; and of men, the Brahmanas . . .
> A Brahmana, coming into existence, is born as the highest on earth, the lord of all created beings, for the protection of the treasury of the law.

And since ritual purity (see above, p. 41) was considered essential for priests, the touch of a ritually impure person (particularly of outcastes) was believed to defile the Brahmana.

Over the centuries, the caste system has become very complicated indeed, with many sub-castes. But the Brahmanas still retain a position of eminence, and are revered by the common people.

In modern India, many of the traditional caste laws have been relaxed. Untouchability has been abolished by law and people who once married entirely within their own caste are now more and more prepared to marry outside it. Although caste is not the force it once was in the higher reaches of Hindu society (particularly among those who have been educated in Western ways), it retains its hold on the mass of the people. Liberals argue that it does not do justice to the equality of men. But against this, it may be pointed out that caste has served as a stabilizing factor in Indian society over the centuries, and that the traditions of Hinduism have been guarded in the caste structure. There is also a sense in which a Hindu is one who has been born as a member of a caste. To lose caste, therefore, is to cease to be a Hindu, — and this, to very many, is still a tragedy.

Rebirth

Almost all Hindus believe that every person has a number of lives to live on earth. This is technically called reincarnation.

An important word connected with this idea is *karma. Karma* means 'works' or 'deeds', and may be regarded simply as a form of credit or debit balance of good or bad deeds. During a normal life each person will be accumulating good or bad *karma* by worshipping God, by showing generosity and mercy, and so on. When a person dies, the soul may pass through a heaven or hell, but only to be reborn. If *karma* has been on the whole good, then it will be reborn at a higher station in life; if bad, at a lower station. The whole cycle of births and rebirths is called *samsara.*

As a man casts off his worn-out clothes
And takes on other new ones [in their place],
So does the embodied soul cast off his worn-out bodies
And enters others new.

This contrasts sharply with the Christian or Jewish belief that each person lives on earth only once.

Belief in reincarnation is often put forward by Hindus as an explanation of the mystery of undeserved suffering. Since a man's or a woman's suffering depends on his balance of good and bad *karma* in a previous existence, *all* suffering is deserved, though not necessarily by wickedness in this present life.

Nevertheless, the ultimate aim of Hinduism as a religion is to achieve salvation. Again, salvation in Hinduism and Christianity are very different ideas. For the Hindu, salvation, *moksha*, means liberation from rebirth (this point is dealt with more thoroughly in Chapter 2).

Under the pressure of western, and particularly Christian, ideas, some Hindus today are no longer prepared to believe fully in reincarnation; but for most it is an unquestioned item of faith.

12. Cows in a street in Madras

The Cow

Most Westerners are unable to understand why the cow should be regarded as sacred by Hindus. The expression 'a sacred cow' is used in a contemptuous sense in English. But the visitor to India soon learns that the cow is a profound symbol to Hindus.

The cow is a symbol of life, of the divine bounty of the earth as the giver of food and nourishment, and as a symbol of the great mother-goddess. Ancient texts speak of the cow as the symbol of all creation. In the *Vishnu Purana* there is a story in which the earth assumes the form of a cow in order to escape Prithu, the monarch of all. She was finally caught and persuaded to nourish the earth with her milk. Then Prithu milked the earth into his own hand, and corn and vegetables grew up for man's food.

It is in the *Bhagavata Purana*, however, that popular reverence for the cow receives its highest expression. In this scripture, which tells of the youth of the god Krishna, the divine lord is depicted as a cow-herd, living the pastoral life among the other herdsmen and herdmaidens of Vrindaban. Thus to worship and reverence the cow is to follow the example of Shri Krishna.

For these reasons the Hindu would never harm a cow, much less kill one or eat its meat. One observer has noted that 'An attempt on the life of the cow at once changes the habitually calm and self-controlled Hindu into a dangerous fanatic.' There are many examples of riots having been started by non-Hindus threatening the life of cows. Unfortunately, 'sacred cows' are not always cared for in India, and particularly in the cities (in 1961 it was estimated that there were more than 175 million cattle in India). The cow, then, can be a problem. But Gandhi's words should be remembered, that:

> 'Cow Protection' to me is one of the most wonderful phenomena in all human evolution; for it takes the human being beyond his species . . . Man through the cow is enjoined to realize his identity with all that lives . . . 'Cow Protection' is the gift of Hinduism to the world; and Hinduism will live as long as there are Hindus to protect the cow.

Vegetarianism

Because the Hindu believes in the sacredness of all life, and that life should on no account be destroyed violently, he is a vegetarian, eating no animal food. If he is orthodox, and particularly if he is a Brahmin, great care must be taken with the preparation of his food, in order not to lose ritual purity. But vegetarianism is a practice followed by almost all Hindus. Hindu restaurants serve only vegetarian food and even on railway stations there are vegetarian snack-bars.

This practice is linked with the doctrine of *ahimsa* (non-violence), as applied to the animal world. Monks belonging to some orders, especially in Jainism, have been in the habit of wearing masks, in order not to kill insects by breathing them in, and of sweeping the path in front of their feet in order to avoid treading on any living creature.

Religious Equality

It is common to find among educated Hindus the belief in the equality of all religions as pathways to God. It may be said, for instance, that adherents of different religions are like pilgrims climbing a hill in the mist, unable to see others climbing the same hill on parallel paths. Only when the summit is reached, and the mist is left behind, can the pilgrims see and recognize one another. Therefore, for a member of one religion to try to persuade others to join him is futile. It may also be unjust, since it is best for a man to remain in the religion in which he was born and brought up. This view was expressed by Ramakrishna (see below, p. 55) in these words:

> A truly religious man should think that other religions also are paths leading to the truth.
> Every man should follow his own religion. A Christian should follow

Christianity, a Muhammadan should follow Muhammadanism, and so on. For the Hindus the ancient path, the path of the Aryan Rishis, is the best.

From this it follows that, although religions are equal in the sight of God, every Indian ought to be Hindu and it is wrong for Christians, say, to attempt to persuade Hindus to become Christians. Under the influence of the Indian national movement, anti-Christian feeling was strong for reasons like these, and although India is a secular state, some states within India have so-called 'anti-conversion laws'.

In practice then, many Hindus will tolerate anything but intolerance. They will, for instance, accept Jesus Christ as divine and as a great teacher (*Jesuswami*), but not as *sole* saviour. Similarly, Muhammad may be accepted as *a* prophet (or *guru*), but not as *the* prophet.

> I maintain that India's great faiths are all-sufficing for her. Apart from Christianity and Judaism, Hinduism and its off-shoots, Islam and Zoroastrianism are living faiths. No one faith is perfect. All faiths are equally dear to their respective votaries. What is wanted, therefore, is living friendly contact among the followers of the great religions of the world, and not a clash among them in the fruitless attempt on the part of each community to show the superiority of its faith over the rest.
> (Gandhi)

An alternative version of this same belief is to say that within all religions there is a core of truth, which all religions have in common; they differ in externals, however, and it is the duty of the believer to penetrate this layer to the truth hidden beneath it, to the Reality which is Brahman. Such is the view of the Vedanta school of philosophy, which sees all phenomena in the world, including the religions, as unreal, or at least as veils hiding Reality, which is one.

These are just some of the points on which many Hindus are of a common mind. It would not be difficult to put forward many more points on which Hindus do not absolutely agree, particularly in the various sects. Those Hindus whom the student is likely to meet in the west will in all probability share these opinions — or most of them.

7

HINDUISM IN THE MODERN WORLD

As times change, religion changes. No religion, even though the idea of the unreality or the impermanence of the world may be part of its teachings, is able to live for very long as though the world around it did not exist. The impact of the modern world on traditional religions has tended to show itself in three ways:

1. More and more people cease to be religious: that is, to be active and committed members of the religious community. This does not mean that they become hostile, but they do become indifferent.
2. Those who *are* active and committed become more so, partly in order to prove that their religion in its traditional form still means something to them and the world, partly in order to combat the influence of the first group.
3. A middle group of so-called liberals develops. These are the people who try to *adapt* their traditional faith to the new situation. They may reject part of their tradition, and because of this are suspected by the second group. They retain another part of it, and are therefore suspected by the first group.

All three are to be found in modern Hinduism. Many intellectuals have turned away almost entirely from traditional religion, although they may still call themselves Hindus ('Hindu' is, as we have seen, a sufficiently flexible term to make this possible). At the other extreme, there are highly con-servative parties which refuse even to consider any change in traditional religion. Sometimes, as in the case of a party called the *Jana Sangh*, political motives are also involved. And in between, there are those, like ex-President Radhakrishnan, who attempt to express traditional values in terms more suited to the twentieth century.

Modern Hinduism dates back about one hundred and fifty years, to the period when the western nations (particularly Britain, but also Portugal and France) were beginning to make a serious impact upon India. Up to this time, about the 1820's, for centuries Hinduism had had to face only one serious challenge — that of Islam. The spread of Islam in India in the eighth century and after had resulted in many Indians becoming Muslims, and had also made many Hindus think more seriously about *one* God as opposed to *many* gods. Of course, some Hindus already believed that God could reveal himself in many ways, and under many forms and names; but Muslims were passionately opposed to image-worship, and taught at least some Hindus to think in the same way.

The coming of the British in the eighteenth century brought to India a new political unity, a new language, and what in most parts of India was a new religion — Christianity. From 1830 on, missionaries and politicians agreed that India should be given the benefit of western-type education in the English language. This soon became popular, and as a result, India had no choice but to receive a large dose of western culture, western science and western values.

This had its effect on Hinduism in two directions. First in the appearance of reform movements which attempted to reach a compromise between east and west; the Brahma (or Brahmo) Samaj is the best known of these. And then, somewhat later, in purely Hindu movements, like the Arya Samaj, which took over certain Western ideas, but remained essentially Indian.

The Brahma Samaj

The Brahma Samaj was founded in 1828 by Raja Ram Mohun Roy (1772–1833). It stressed the worship of one God (Brahma) in forms reminiscent of Islam and Christianity, and opposed idolatry. It also fought for social reform within India, and Ram Mohun Roy was instrumental in bringing about the abolition of *sati* (widow-burning, see above, p. 44). He helped the Scottish missionary Alexander Duff to establish the first Christian centre of higher education in Calcutta (1830), and some years earlier had published a book called *The Precepts of Jesus: The Guide to Peace and Happiness.* Nevertheless he remained a convinced Hindu. On his death (in England), his society fell upon hard times; later leaders were unable to hold it together, and its influence gradually declined. Its policy of compromise was no longer acceptable in a nationally aware India, and the decline of the Brahma Samaj corresponded closely to the growth of the national movement in the years after about 1880.

The Arya Samaj

The Arya Samaj was founded in 1875 by Swami Dayananda Sarasvati (1824–83), and aimed from the first at recalling Hindus to traditional ways of thought, based on the Vedas:

> It has become the spearhead of a dynamic type of Hinduism, trying to unify all sections of Hindu society, reclaiming those who have gone out of the fold, making new converts, and fighting all enemies who make inroads into the Vedic religion. It takes its stand on the Vedas and the Vedas alone, and ignores all the later developments; thus it denounces idol worship and the caste system. Curiously enough, it takes little account of the philosophy of the Upanishads, and consequently cuts itself off from the perennial sources of Hindu religious thought. Therefore the Samaj has become more a school of nationalism than of religion proper.

It is not without significance that the Arya Samaj has always been strongest in Hindi-speaking north and west India, i.e., in those areas where the national movement has been strongest. Its Aryan (Sanskrit) basis has never appealed to the South of India.

The Theosophical Society

The Theosophical Society was also founded in 1875 by Madame Blavatsky and Col. Olcott. Its outstanding leader in India was, however, Mrs. Annie Besant (1847–1933), an Englishwoman who had came to India in 1893. Theosophical teachings as such are of little significance, but under Mrs. Besant the Society developed an extensive programme of publishing in the area of Hindu scriptures, and she started the college which has since grown into the Benares Hindu University.

Shri Ramakrishna

Ramakrishna (1836–86) has been described as 'a living synthesis of all religions'. He was a poor, unlearned *pujari* at a Calcutta temple, but undoubtedly one of the great religious geniuses of modern times.

In his quest for Reality, he was led to practise Muslim and Christian disciplines, as well as those of his own tradition – that of the worship of Kali as Divine Mother. It has been said that his appetite for spiritual experience in all its forms was insatiable.

Ramakrishna taught, on the basis of his own experience, that the outward forms of any religion are unimportant, compared to the unity which they all express inwardly. And the truly religious person, whether he be Hindu, Muslim or Christian, can pass through these outward forms to the experience of Reality, which is always and everywhere the same. It is doubtful, however, whether Ramakrishna would be known today, were it not for two men: Mahendranath, who compiled the collection of sayings now known as *The Gospel of Shri Ramakrishna*; and Swami Vivekananda.

Swami Vivekananda

On Ramakrishna's death, a group of his followers joined together to form what was later to be called the *Ramakrishna Mission.* Among its leaders, Swami Vivekananda (1863–1902) was outstanding, both as an organizer and as a teacher. In 1893, he visited America to take part in the Chicago World's Parliament of Religions, and on his return to India, after four highly successful years touring, he was hailed as Hinduism's first missionary to the west. His message was substantially that of Ramakrishna: that all religions are ways to the one Supreme Reality, but he also learned from the west the value of social action, and founded schools, colleges and hospitals.

Today, a Ramakrishna Mission centre has all these things, as well as a meditation room containing an image of Ramakrishna and murals depicting all the great religious leaders of mankind. There are such centres in all the main Indian cities, and in many places in the west. The view of religion which Ramakrishna and Vivekananda taught is now accepted by very many Hindus, even though they may not be actively connected with the movement. In 1893 Vivekananda said that:

> . . . if there is ever to be a universal religion it must be one which will hold no location in place or time; which will be infinite, like the god it will preach; whose sun shines upon the followers of Krishna or Christ, saints or sinners, alike; which will not be in the Brahmin or Buddhist, Christian or Muhammadan, but the sum total of all these, and still have infinite space for development, which in its catholicity will embrace in its infinite arms and find a place for every human being . . .

Hinduism, he taught, contained the essence of that religion.

Other Leaders

Hinduism has been rich in leaders this century. Shri Aurobindo Ghose (1872–1950) was an outstanding nationalist leader earlier this century, who withdrew from public life, founded an *ashram* (retreat centre) and wrote many books, the best known being *The Life Divine*. Rabindranath

13. Gandhi at a reception given by Rabindranath Tagore

Tagore (1861–1941), the son of one of the early leaders of the Brahma Samaj, was a great mystical poet in the *bhakti* tradition, and was awarded the Nobel Prize for Literature in 1913, mainly for his *Gitanjali* (Song Offerings), from which these words are taken:

> Let only that little be left of me whereby I may name thee my all.
> Let only that little be left of my will whereby I may feel thee on every side, and come to thee in everything, and offer thee my love every moment.

Sarvepalli Radhakrishnan (b. 1888) is known throughout the world as India's greatest philosopher this century, as an Oxford Professor, and as President of India. In all these capacities he has been, by teaching and example, one of Hinduism's greatest advocates since Vivekananda. His book *The Hindu View of Life* is probably the most capable piece of Hindu apologetics ever written.

14. 'Mahatma' Gandhi

Mohandas Karamchand Gandhi

But no modern Hindu leader can approach M. K. 'Mahatma' Gandhi (1869–1948) in influence. He it was who led India to independence, though it is worth noting that his assassin was a member of a right-wing Hindu movement that believed Gandhi to have betrayed India. Gandhi was a social reformer, but his actions as a social reformer were fundamentally religious. He claimed only to be wearing the mask of a politician. His teachings were centred on three ideas:

Satyagraha (soul-force, or truth-force), the holding fast to truth in face of all opposition;

Ahimsa (non-violence), the expression of love and humility as well as pacifism;

Brahmacharya (discipleship), the expression of continence, fasting (when necessary) and inward discipline.

His autobiography, *The Story of my Experiments with Truth*, is world-famous.

To select a single quotation from his writings is hard, but these words are typical:

In order to attain a perfect fellowship, every act of its members must be a religious act and an act of sacrifice. I came to the conclusion long ago, after prayerful search and study and discussion with as many people as I could meet, that all religions are true and, also, that all had some error in them; and that whilst I hold by my own, I should hold others as dear as Hinduism; from which it logically follows that we should hold all as dear as our nearest kith and kin and that we should make no distinction between them. So, we can only pray, if we are Hindus, not that a Christian should become a Hindu; or if we are Mussulmans [Muslims], not that a Hindu or a Christian should become a Mussulman; nor should we even secretly pray that anyone should be converted; but our inward prayer should be that a Hindu should be a better Hindu, a Muslim a better Muslim and a Christian a better Christian. That is the fundamental truth of fellowship.

Gandhi's work has been of very great inspiration to many people all over the world; Martin Luther King in America may serve as an example. In India, while it may be true that he has more admirers than imitators, there would be few Hindus who would not agree with the words quoted above, or with D. S. Sarma, who wrote that Gandhi 'is generally considered to be one of the greatest saints that ever lived'.

To understand Gandhi is in a very real sense to understand Hinduism in the twentieth century, and to understand India.

Postscript

We have been looking together at something of the history of Hinduism, and at a few of its more important beliefs and practices. There is much more which might have been said, and much more which we might all study. Let us remember, though, that in all this, we are dealing with people, and with the way of life of one of the greatest of the nations of the world.

India today is called a secular state, which means that all religions (and there are many of them) are respected equally. But this does not mean that all the people of India respect one another equally.

In this sense, India is the world in miniature. There are many religions (and anti-religions) in the world, and if there is to be mutual respect and tolerance between peoples, there must be mutual understanding. Religion cannot and must not be ignored or despised. Rather, the religions of mankind must be studied with care and sympathy, in order that such mutual understanding may grow. If we are ever to be united, we must love one another; if we are to love one another, we must know and understand one another; if we are to know and understand one another, we must meet one another, openly and without impatience or fear.

To understand India and Hinduism, then, may be a key to the better understanding of the world in which we live.